GEORGIA O'KEEFFE

Desert Painter

Emily Rose Kucharczyk

BLACKBIRCH PRESS

THOMSON

GALE

Detroit • New York • San Diego • San Francisco
Boston • New Haven, Conn. • Waterville, Maine
London • Munich

Published by Blackbirch Press
10911 Technology Place
San Diego, CA 92127
e-mail: customerservice@galegroup.com
Web site: http://www.galegroup.com/blackbirch

© 2002 Blackbirch Press
an imprint of the Gale Group

Printed in China

10 9 8 7 6 5 4 3 2 1

Photo credits:
Cover © Bettmann/CORBIS; page 4-5 © State Historical Society of Wisconsin; page 6 © National Gallery of Art; page 8-9 © Bettmann/CORBIS; page 10-11 © Corel; page 12-13 © The Library of Congress; page 14-15 © CORBIS; page 16 © The Metropolitan Museum of Art, Alfred Stieglitz Collection, 1955; page 18-19 © The Metropolitan Museum of Art, Alfred Stieglitz Collection, 1963. Photograph by Malcolm Varon; page 20 © The Art Institute of Chicago, Alfred Stieglitz Collection, 1949; page 22, 27 © The Metropolitan Museum of Art, Alfred Stieglitz Collection 1969. Photograph by Malcolm Varon; page 23 © Brooklyn Museum of Art; page 24 © The Metropolitan Museum of Art, Gift of David A. Schulte, 1928; page 25 © property of Blackbirch Press; page 26 © The Metropolitan Museum of Art, Alfred Stieglitz Collection, 1950. Photograph by Malcolm Varon; page 28 © The Metropolitan Museum of Art, Alfred Stieglitz Collection, 1959. Photograph by Malcolm Varon; page 29 © Bettmann/CORBIS; page 30 © Dan Budnik/Woodfin Camp.

Library of Congress Cataloging-in-Publication Data
Kucharczyk, Emily Rose.
Georgia O'Keeffe / by Emily Rose Kucharczyk.
        p. cm. — (Famous women juniors)
Includes index.
Summary: Introduces the life of the painter whose fame came to rest with her large works from nature.
        ISBN 1-56711-592-6 (alk. paper)
1. O'Keeffe, Georgia, 1887-1986—Juvenile literature. 2. Painters—United States—Biography—Juvenile literature. 3. O'Keeffe, Georgia, 1887-1986—Juvenile literature.
[1. O'Keeffe, Georgia, 1887-1986. 2. Artists. 3. Women—Biography.] I. Title. II. Series.
ND237.05 K83 2002
759.13—dc21   2001005069

Prairie Life

Georgia O'Keeffe was a famous artist. She painted large pictures of flowers, shells, bones, and other objects from nature.

Georgia was born in Sun Prairie, Wisconsin, on November 15, 1887. Her parents were farmers. Georgia's father, Frank, liked nature and enjoyed traveling. Georgia's mother, Ida Totto, loved to read and play the piano. Georgia had four sisters and two brothers. All the children helped out on the family farm.

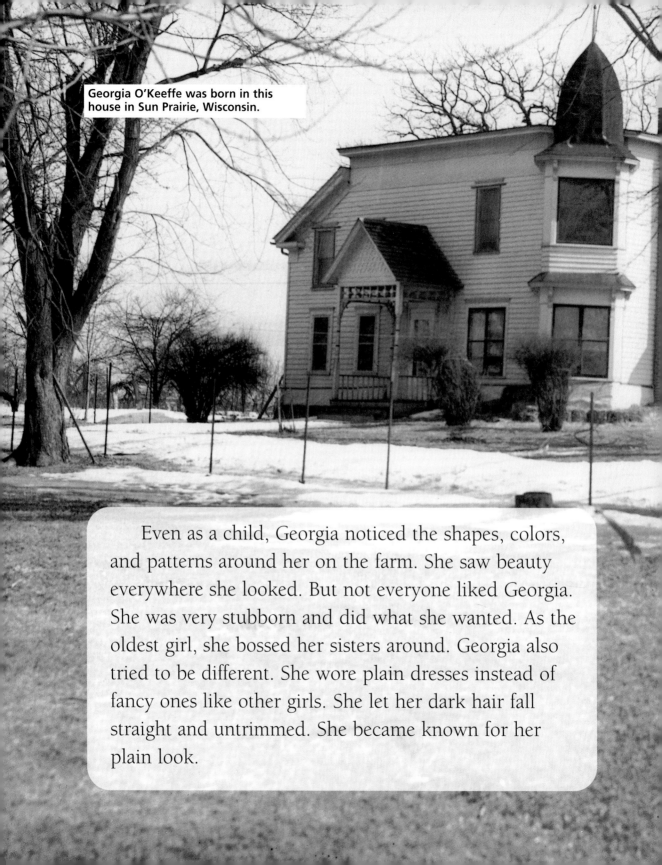

Georgia O'Keeffe was born in this house in Sun Prairie, Wisconsin.

Even as a child, Georgia noticed the shapes, colors, and patterns around her on the farm. She saw beauty everywhere she looked. But not everyone liked Georgia. She was very stubborn and did what she wanted. As the oldest girl, she bossed her sisters around. Georgia also tried to be different. She wore plain dresses instead of fancy ones like other girls. She let her dark hair fall straight and untrimmed. She became known for her plain look.

Georgia liked to spend time alone. She let her imagination keep her company. In between chores—such as cooking, sewing, hoeing, and weeding—she played games and swung on the two big swings behind the barn.

Georgia especially enjoyed playing with dolls. Her dollhouse was two thin boards slit halfway down that fit together like a cross. She pretended the boards made four inside rooms. Georgia set up the dollhouse outside. She cut patches of grass to make a lawn for the house. She used a dishpan filled with water as a lake.

Georgia did not like regular school. Luckily, however, her mother made all the children take private music and drawing lessons. Georgia loved the lessons.

Georgia worked hard to improve her drawing. She never gave up. One time she tried to draw a man bending over, but could not make his knees bend the right way. She solved the problem by turning the paper around so the man lay on his back with his legs in the air. She was always able to look at things in a way others did not.

As Georgia and her sisters became more skilled at drawing, Mrs. O'Keeffe wanted them to learn to paint. One Saturday each month they took a seven-mile trip to study with Sarah Mann. Mann had her students copy pictures from books in watercolor. Georgia was not happy with her copies. She thought they did not look enough like the originals.

Soon, Georgia was painting at home and using lively color. Georgia's mother noticed her daughter's talent, and hoped Georgia would become an art teacher. No one thought she would become an artist. People at that time thought that the life of an artist was too free-spirited for girls.

Georgia felt differently. In eighth grade she told her friend Lena, "I'm going to be an artist."

Georgia entered a Catholic school in Madison, Wisconsin, when she was 14. She took art lessons with Sister Angelique. For her first assignment, Georgia worked on a charcoal drawing of a baby's hand. Georgia thought it was good, but her teacher said it was too small and messy. Sister Angelique told Georgia that she should use large, light lines instead of small, dark ones. Drawing large pictures opened a new world to Georgia. She decided that she would never draw little pictures again. Soon she was the best art student in her class.

The next year, 1902, Georgia and her older brother, Francis, went to high school in the city of Milwaukee. One day, her new art teacher brought in a flower and told the students to draw it. Suddenly Georgia realized that she could draw pictures of everyday objects instead of simply copying the paintings of other artists. She began to pay more attention to details. Sometimes she only drew part of a flower, like a petal.

Madison, Wisconsin, around 1900.
Georgia entered private school here
at the age of 14.

A New Home

While Georgia was at school, her parents decided to sell their farm in Wisconsin and move to Williamsburg, Virginia. They bought a house and a general store.

The weather in Williamsburg was warmer than in Wisconsin, and there were many flowering trees. Georgia liked to hike in the woods and look at the colors and shapes that surrounded her.

In 1903, Georgia entered the Chatham Episcopal Institute, a private school in the Blue Ridge Mountains of western Virginia. She was popular and friendly, even though she was different from the other girls. She liked to play tricks and try daring stunts. She even taught her classmates how to play poker.

Teachers and students noticed Georgia's artistic talent right away. Soon she was allowed to use the school art room all the time. But Georgia did poorly in other school subjects. She barely passed. Before she graduated, Georgia had to take a spelling test six times. She needed to spell at least 75 out of 100 words correctly. Finally, after six tries, she spelled 76 words properly. Georgia graduated in 1905.

In September, 17-year-old Georgia entered the Art Institute of Chicago. She lived with her Aunt Ollie, who worked at a newspaper. Aunt Ollie was one of the few women newspaper reporters at the time.

Georgia was nervous about going to the Art Institute. The school was very big, and she did not like the classes because she didn't get to experiment with color. Students had to copy European paintings and were judged on their work every week. Those who did well got to move their easels closer to the front of the room. Even though she wasn't happy, Georgia moved to the front quickly and became the best student in her class.

Georgia entered the Art Institute of Chicago at age 17.

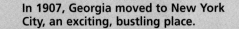
In 1907, Georgia moved to New York City, an exciting, bustling place.

During her first summer vacation, Georgia caught a serious illness—typhoid fever. She was still recovering from the illness when school started, so she stayed at home in Virginia.

In the fall of 1907, one of Georgia's former art teachers encouraged her to attend the Art Students League in New York. The O'Keeffes scraped together the money and Georgia went to New York City. It was an exciting place for a young artist. Trains, trolleys, and subways were replacing horse-drawn buggies, and skyscrapers were being built.

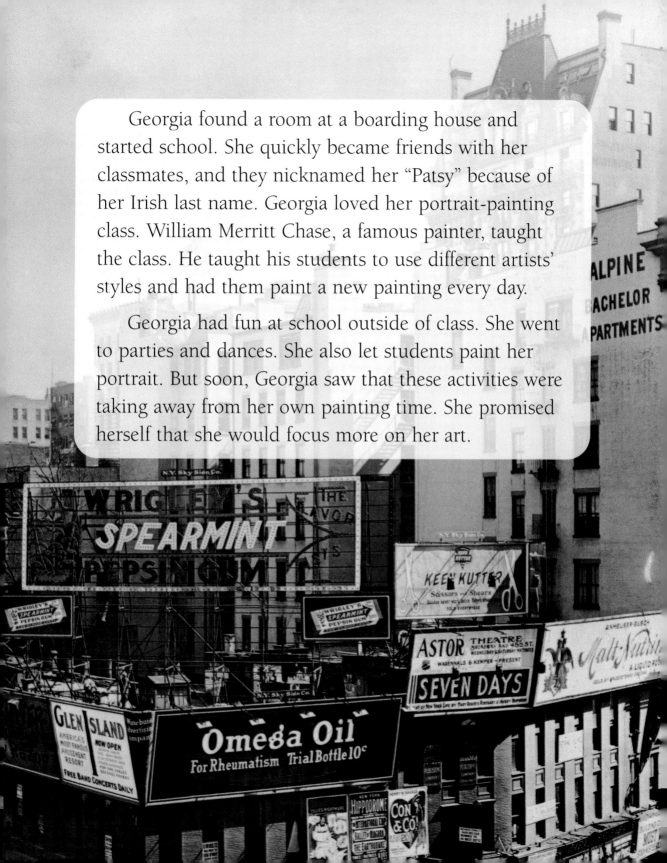

Georgia found a room at a boarding house and started school. She quickly became friends with her classmates, and they nicknamed her "Patsy" because of her Irish last name. Georgia loved her portrait-painting class. William Merritt Chase, a famous painter, taught the class. He taught his students to use different artists' styles and had them paint a new painting every day.

Georgia had fun at school outside of class. She went to parties and dances. She also let students paint her portrait. But soon, Georgia saw that these activities were taking away from her own painting time. She promised herself that she would focus more on her art.

During this time, Georgia met Alfred Stieglitz, a photographer. He owned a gallery called 291 in New York, where he exhibited new, unusual art. Georgia had never seen such exciting modern art before.

At the end of her first year at school, Georgia won a scholarship to attend a summer art program in upstate New York. She began to develop her own style there. It was a style that came from deep inside her. She learned to paint with emotion. She noticed that how she felt affected how she painted.

In New York, Georgia met Alfred Stieglitz, a photographer and gallery owner.

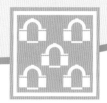

Georgia returned to Williamsburg when the program was over. Her family now had more serious money problems, so she was unable to return to school. Instead, in the fall of 1908, she boarded a train to Chicago and went to live with her Aunt Ollie again. Georgia got a job drawing household products for newspaper ads.

While in Chicago, Georgia got the measles. In 1909, she went home to Virginia. Her father's business was falling apart and her mother was sick. Georgia had to take care of her family. By 1911, Georgia had lost all hope of going back to school and becoming a painter. She said she was going to give up painting.

A New Direction

In the spring, Elizabeth Willis, Georgia's former art teacher at Chatham, asked her to teach a class. Georgia was a good teacher and liked working with young people.

In 1912, Georgia returned to painting and took classes with Alon Bement. He told her to paint using her feelings. He said instead of just painting a flower, she should paint the way the flower made her feel. It was a style that Georgia had discovered several summers earlier. Georgia started to enjoy painting again.

This landscape was painted in the 1930s.

She needed to earn money, however, so she took a job teaching art in Amarillo, Texas. Georgia took her students for walks on the prairie and had them draw what they saw. She wanted them to enjoy the beauty all around them. Georgia also enjoyed the open desert spaces of Texas.

Georgia returned to Virginia when the school year was over. She wanted to earn a teaching degree, but didn't have enough money to pay for school. Aunt Ollie offered to pay for her to attend Columbia Teachers' College in New York City. At 27, Georgia returned to New York.

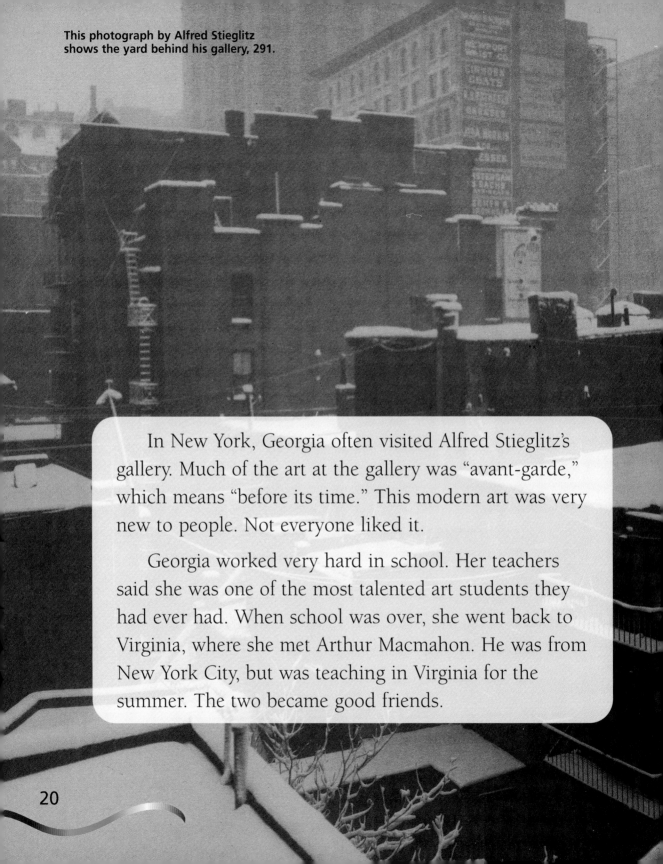

This photograph by Alfred Stieglitz shows the yard behind his gallery, 291.

In New York, Georgia often visited Alfred Stieglitz's gallery. Much of the art at the gallery was "avant-garde," which means "before its time." This modern art was very new to people. Not everyone liked it.

Georgia worked very hard in school. Her teachers said she was one of the most talented art students they had ever had. When school was over, she went back to Virginia, where she met Arthur Macmahon. He was from New York City, but was teaching in Virginia for the summer. The two became good friends.

Arthur went back to New York when the summer was over, but Georgia couldn't because she didn't have enough money. She missed Arthur a lot.

Georgia found a job at a small school in South Carolina. During the Christmas holiday there, she worked on a series of charcoal drawings. The shapes showed curving lines and sharp forms. They were filled with emotion and energy. They showed how she felt about Arthur.

Georgia sent the drawings to her friend Anita Pollitzer in New York. She asked Anita not to show them to anyone. But Anita liked them so much she brought them to Alfred Stieglitz. He was amazed by the drawings and hung ten of them in his gallery in the spring of 1916.

Georgia finally found a way to return to school in New York. She did not know that her drawings were being exhibited.

Georgia's painting *Blue Lines* was exhibited in 1916.

When she found out, she was angry, and demanded that Stieglitz take them down. He refused because he thought the world should see her art. Finally, she agreed to let him keep her drawings on display.

Soon after Georgia had returned to school, Mrs. O'Keeffe died. Georgia had to leave New York to be with her family. She waited many weeks after her mother's death before she painted again. Her new paintings were full of sad feelings. They were all blue and abstract (not meant to look like or represent something). Georgia sent her paintings to Stieglitz.

Stieglitz liked Georgia's work so much that he gave her a show at his gallery. She sold her first painting there for $400.

This painting, *Blue Number 2,* reflects Georgia's sadness about her mother's death.

Not all critics liked her work. Some critics said her paintings were "full of risks." She soon earned a reputation as a daring and dramatic artist who loved to use color.

Alfred Stieglitz made this portrait of Georgia in 1918.

Meanwhile, Georgia got a job teaching in Canyon, Texas. The townspeople had never met anyone like her before. They noticed that she always wore black and looked plain. She roamed the desert and brought back objects for her students to paint. She was inspired by the colorful landscape and began to paint with different colors again.

In 1917, the United States entered World War I. Young men were encouraged to drop out of school and join the army to fight against the Germans. Georgia thought that her students should stay in school. Many people thought she was unpatriotic for feeling that way.

Many Americans hated anyone who was German or who had relatives who were from Germany. Georgia thought it was wrong to hate people because of their nationality. Soon, Georgia felt unwelcome in the town.

Georgia became ill and went to a friend's ranch to get better. Alfred Stieglitz was worried about her and sent for Georgia to come back to New York. She left Texas for New York in June 1918.

This painting depicts soldiers during World War I.

Back in New York

Georgia and Alfred soon fell in love. Alfred separated from his wife to be with Georgia.

Georgia painted every day. People wanted to buy her work, but she had a difficult time giving up her paintings. Each work was special to her. In 1923, she had another show that Alfred arranged. Thousands of people came to the show to see her paintings of landscapes and flowers.

By now, Georgia's paintings had become more abstract, with colors that were deeper and more

This painting, *Corn Dark I*, was done in 1924, the same year Georgia married Alfred Stieglitz.

intense. She painted huge pictures of flowers close up. So close, that it was like being inside a flower.

Alfred and Georgia were finally married in 1924. As years passed, Georgia felt trapped in her personal life. She wanted to visit new places and find new things to paint. She went on a trip to New Mexico with a friend. She enjoyed the bright desert colors and clean air. She was happy when she returned to New York.

Black Iris III was one of Georgia's early flower painting.

But life in New York City had changed. New York felt gray and closed in to her, and her paintings during this time showed that. She was having a hard time thinking of new paintings. Georgia left Alfred and went back to New Mexico the next summer.

Finally, Georgia couldn't stand living in two places. She became sick with horrible headaches and chest pains. She was angry and depressed. She took her suffering out on her sister Catherine, who was also a painter. Georgia thought Catherine's paintings were too much like her own. She sent Catherine an angry letter threatening to tear up all her paintings. Catherine never painted after that. Georgia stayed in the hospital for more than six months. She had stopped painting.

When she recovered, she moved to New Mexico. She wanted to be alone. Georgia began painting again in New Mexico. She painted red and gray hills and cliffs, stones, flowers, and animal bones.

Thousands of people came to see her work at Stieglitz's gallery in New York. Her paintings were

Georgia often painted animal bones and skulls. The name of this painting is *From the Faraway Nearby*.

selling for $5,000 each.

In 1946, Alfred collapsed in his gallery in New York. A few days later he died at age 82.

Georgia spent the next 20 years traveling, entertaining guests, becoming involved in her community, and painting. She especially liked painting views of the sky.

Alfred Stieglitz, later in life, stands next to some of Georgia's paintings.

Georgia bought a run-down ranch near Abiquiu, New Mexico, and hired townspeople to help her with her house. She donated money to the town to build a gym for kids, and paid for a clean drinking water system for the town. She donated money to help build a school and gave children money to go to the movies. She even paid some of the teenagers' college tuitions.

At the age of 80, Georgia lost some of her eyesight and became depressed. She could no longer paint as well as she had. Then she met a young man named Juan Hamilton. He was a potter, and taught her how to make hand-thrown pots. He encouraged her to paint again, and she did.

When Georgia became too ill to live on her ranch, she moved to Santa Fe, where she died in 1986 at the age of 98. She is still known today as one of America's greatest artists. Her colorful and passionate paintings are unlike those of any other painter.

Georgia befriended Juan Hamilton late in her life.

Glossary

Artist A person who creates something by using imagination and creative skill.

Exhibit To show or display.

Gallery A building or room devoted to displaying works of art.

Portrait A picture representing a person, usually showing the person's face.

Talent A special or creative, natural skill.

Typhoid A disease caused by bacteria; symptoms include fever and chills.

For More Information

Websites

www.okeeffemuseum.org/indexflash.html
The Georgia O'Keeffe Museum
This official website offers a biography of the artist, prints online, and information on upcoming exhibits.

www.ellensplace.net/okeeffe1.html
Georgia O'Keeffe
Georgia's life with Steiglitz as well as her life as a young artist is detailed.

Books

Brooks, Phillip. *Georgia O'Keeffe: An Adventurous Spirit.* Danbury, CT: Franklin Watts, 1995.

Turner, Robyn Montana. *Georgia O'Keeffe (Portraits of Women Artists for Children).* Boston: Little, Brown, and Company Children's Book Division, 1993.

Winter, Jeanette. *My Name is Georgia: A Portrait.* New York: Harcourt Trade Division, 1998.

Index